Orang-utans

by Helen Orme

ticktock

Copyright © ticktock Entertainment Ltd 2006
First published in Great Britain in 2006 by ticktock Media Ltd.,
Unit 2, Orchard Business Centre, North Farm Road,
Tunbridge Wells, Kent, TN2 3XF
ISBN 1 86007 962 8 pbk
Printed in Hong Kong
A CIP catalogue record for this book is available from the British Library.

We would like to thank our consultant Dr. Gary Shapiro Ph.D.
Vice President, Orangutan Foundation International

Picture credits
t=top, b=bottom, c=centre, l-left, r=right
Alamy: 12-13, 15, 16-17, 24-25. Corbis: 10-11, 22-23, 25t. Digital Vision: OFC, 4-5, 8, 9, 10-11, 14, 22-23, 24, 25bl,
26, 27, 28, 31, 32. FLPA: 7c, 25br. Orangutan Foundation UK: 29.
Every effort has been made to trace the copyright holders, and we apologise in advance for any unintentional omissions.
We would be pleased to insert the appropriate acknowledgements in any subsequent edition of this publication.

CONTENTS

Words that appear **in bold** are explained in the glossary.

THE WORLD OF THE ORANG-UTAN

*Orang-utans are large tree-living **apes**. They live in **rainforests** on the islands of Sumatra and Borneo in South East Asia.*

Female orang-utans usually have just one baby at a time.

Baby orang-utans have a lot to learn. For the first seven years of their life, their mothers will teach them all they need to know about living in the rainforest.

ADULT ORANG-UTANS

Adult orang-utans live alone. Each orang-utan has its own **territory** *in the rainforest.*

Males and females only meet for mating.

Male orang-utans often fight if another male comes near.

Male orang-utans look quite different from females. They are nearly twice as big, and have large cheek pouches at the sides of their faces.

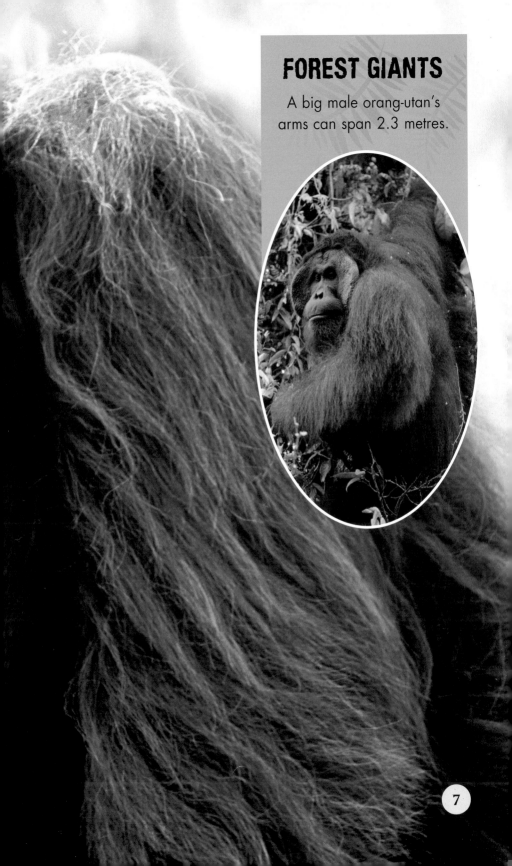

FOREST GIANTS

A big male orang-utan's arms can span 2.3 metres.

THE HUNT FOR FOOD

Orang-utans need to travel long distances through the rainforest to find their food.

They mostly travel above the ground, using their powerful arms to swing from one branch to another.

Orang-utans eat many different sorts of food, such as fruit and leaves, birds' eggs, snails and **termites**.

BABY FOOD FACT

For the first few months, baby orang-utans only drink their mother's milk. Later, they eat fruit which is chewed and softened for them by their mother.

NIGHT IN THE FOREST

*At night the rainforest is full of the sounds of insects and **nocturnal** creatures, such as lorises.*

Orang-utans build sleeping nests high up in the forks of trees.

These nests are made by bending branches into a bowl shape. The orang-utans fill the bowl with leaves to make it soft and snug.

Lorises are small, tree-living animals with thick fur.

RAINFOREST IN DANGER

The biggest threat facing the orang-utan is the destruction of the rainforest.

The islands where orang-utans live are crowded with people. Many people are poor. Cutting timber from the forest is often the only way they can earn enough to live.

In some places there are laws to protect the forest. But because there are not enough people to enforce the laws, the **logging** is not stopped.

WHY ARE THE TREES CUT DOWN?

• Rainforest trees are cut down for timber or to be made into paper.

• Gold has been found in the rainforest. Trees are cut down to make room for gold mines.

• People need farmland to grow food.

POACHERS

Some people kill or capture orang-utans.
This is called poaching.

In the past, some orang-utans were killed for food.
Now the poaching problem has become much worse
because many people want baby orang-utans for pets.

The poachers treat the orang-utans very cruelly.
Often the mother is killed to make it easier to take
the baby.

Many baby orang-utans die before they reach their
new owners.

ORANG-UTANS FOR SALE

Baby orang-utans can be sold for a lot of money. But this does not mean that they are well looked after by the poachers.

They are often put into tiny cages and sold at markets by the side of the road. Sometimes they are not fed properly.

RESCUE CENTRES

Orang-utans do not make good pets. When they become adults, they are very strong and can be bad tempered.

When people get tired of their pet orang-utans, many of the animals are killed.

The lucky ones might go to a rescue centre. Here they are looked after until they are ready to live by themselves, back in the rainforest.

At rescue centres vets check the orang-utans to make sure they have not picked up a disease while they have been living with humans.

TEACHING ORANG-UTANS TO BE WILD

In the wild, young orang-utans learn what food is safe to eat, and where to find it. They also learn how to travel through the rainforest and how to stay safe.

Babies that have been kept as pets do not know how to do these things.

The rescue centre carers start to teach
the babies by putting food on feeding
platforms up in the rainforest trees.

Slowly, the young orang-utans will
learn where to find their own food.

PROTECTING THE ORANG-UTANS

*The rescued orang-utans are released into **nature reserves**.*

Forest rangers patrol the reserves and loggers and poachers are not allowed into these areas.

But there are still problems. Governments of the countries where orang-utans live cannot afford to pay for enough rangers to make sure that the animals are safe.

Outside the reserves, orang-utans are not protected at all, and their **habitat** is disappearing fast.

EXTINCTION

Unless a lot more is done to protect them, scientists say that orang-utans could become **extinct** in the wild in just ten years.

FACTFILE

WHERE DO ORANG-UTANS LIVE?

Orang-utans are found on the islands of Sumatra and Borneo in South East Asia.

SOUTH EAST ASIA

• The orang-utans' habitat is being destroyed. Now they only live in the places shown in red on the main map.

MALAYSIA

PACIFIC OCEAN

BORNEO

SUMATRA

INDONESIA

JAVA

• Orang-utans live high in the rainforest trees about 30 metres above the ground.

The name orang-utan means 'person of the forest' in the Malay language.

ORANG-UTAN BODIES

Orang-utans are the largest tree-living animals in the world.

• An adult male orang-utan has leathery cheek pouches.

• The red fur of the orang-utan is a perfect **camouflage** in the rainforest. In the green light, they are almost impossible to see from the ground.

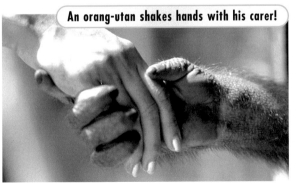

An orang-utan shakes hands with his carer!

Female

Height: up to 1 m
Weight: 50 kg

Male

Height: up to 1.4 m
Weight: 90 kg

• An orang-utan's hand is like the hand of a human. It is designed to be able to hold things. Their feet can do this, too!

25

BABY ORANG-UTANS

A baby orang-utan holds on to mum.

- Orang-utans weigh less than two kilograms when they are born.

- Mother orang-utans carry their babies around until they are about three years old.

- A baby orang-utan drinks its mother's milk until it is about five years old.

ORANG-UTAN FOOD

- Orang-utans eat over 400 different types of food. They eat figs, durian fruit, leaves, bark, birds' eggs, snails, ants and termites.

- Orang-utans do not come to the ground for water. They find small puddles where branches meet tree trunks, or they lick water from leaves.

The spiny durian fruit tastes sweet and cheesy!

FACTFILE

ORANG-UTAN LIFE

- Adult orang-utans live alone. The fathers do not help to bring up the babies.

- Adult male orang-utans call to warn other males to stay away from their territories. Their cheek pouches make their calls louder. The sound can be heard from a kilometre away.

- Orang-utans use leaves to wipe themselves clean after a meal, as cups to scoop up water, and even as umbrellas!

- In the wild, orang-utans can live to be forty years old.

ORANG-UTANS IN DANGER

*There are probably only 25,000 orang-utans left in the wild.
Ten years ago there were twice as many.*

DISAPPEARING RAINFOREST

• In the last 20 years, 80% of the rainforest where the orang-utans live has been cut down for timber or paper-making, or to make room for farms and gold mines.

Forest fires have destroyed large areas of rainforest.

• Logging is often against the law, but nothing is done to stop it.

• Roads have been made through the rainforest. This makes it easier for poachers and loggers to come into the forest.

• Forest fires are started to clear areas of forest, but they often spread out of control.

• Each orang-utan needs a large territory to find enough to eat. The small areas of forest left are not big enough to support a large number of orang-utans.

KILLING AND POACHING

• Poachers take baby orang-utans from their mothers and sell them as pets. Often the mother is killed.

• Poaching is a serious problem because female orang-utans only have two or three babies in their whole life.

• Out of every ten babies captured, eight or nine will die before they reach their new owner.

• Loggers and other people working in the rainforest sometimes kill orang-utans for food. This is known as 'bush meat'.

• Sometimes, orang-utans steal crops and farmers will kill them.

A baby orang-utan rescued from poachers.

HELPING ORANG-UTANS

• Rescue workers set up centres to care for young orang-utans who do not have a mother to look after them.

• The carers try to teach the young animals how to live in the rainforest.

• **Conservationists** help governments to set up special reserves where logging and mining are not allowed.

HOW YOU CAN HELP

• Join a group that helps orang-utans such as the *Orangutan Foundation UK* (see below) and help them raise money for their work.

• Make sure that any wood your family buys has the FSC label (Forest Stewardship Council). This means the wood has not come from loggers who are breaking the law. • Buy recycled paper.

**Visit these websites for more information
and to find out how
you can help to 'Save the orang-utan'.**

Orangutan Foundation UK: www.orangutan.org.uk

*The Borneo Orangutan Survival Foundation:
www.savetheorangutan.com*

Sepilok Orangutan Appeal UK: www.orangutan-appeal.org.uk

GLOSSARY

apes A group of mammals that includes orang-utans, chimpanzees, gorillas and humans.

camouflage Fur or skin that makes an animal hard to see in the place where it lives.

conservationists People who take care of the natural world. Conservationists try to stop people hunting endangered animals and they ask governments to pass laws to protect wild habitats.

extinct When a type of animal or plant completely disappears.

forest rangers People whose job it is to look after protected nature reserves and the animals that live there. They work for governments and sometimes for conservation organisations.

habitat The place that suits a particular animal or plant in the wild.

logging Cutting down trees for wood.

nature reserves Protected areas where the killing of animals or the cutting down of trees is against the law.

nocturnal When an animal is only active at night.

rainforests Warm, wet places where lots of trees and plants grow. Many animals, such as monkeys, gibbons and clouded leopards, live in the rainforests where the orang-utans live.

termites Insects a bit like ants that live in large groups.

territory The area in which an animal or a family of animals lives.

INDEX